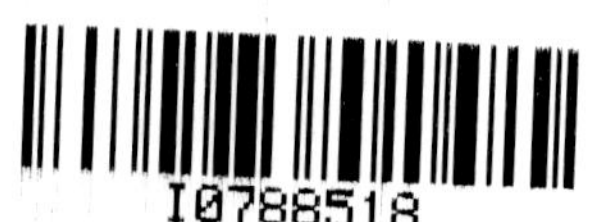

This book belongs to

a Paul Doodles original

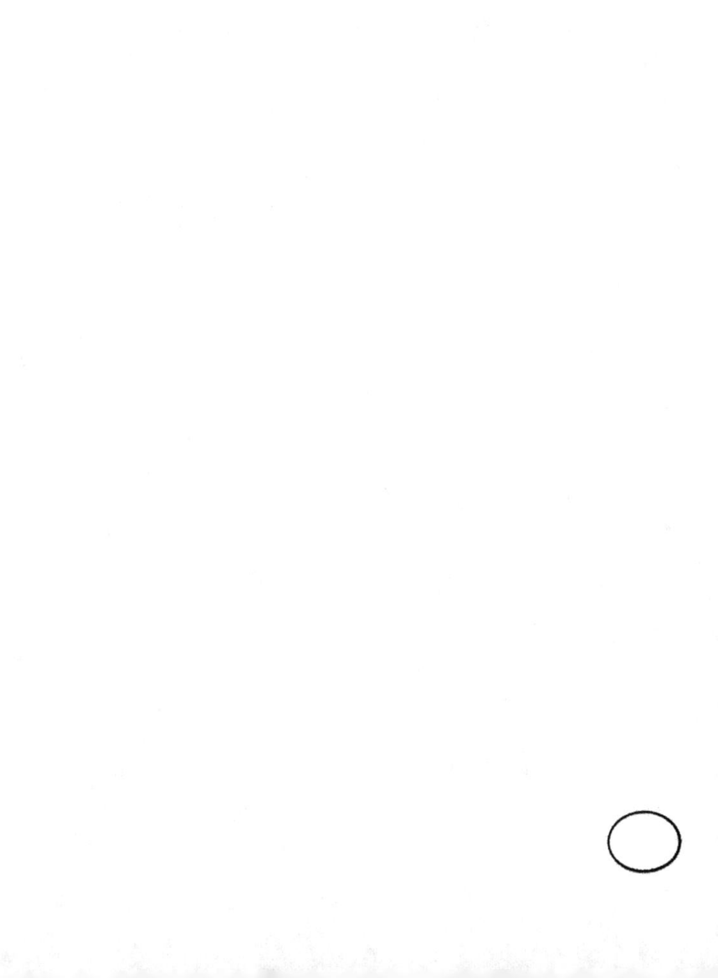

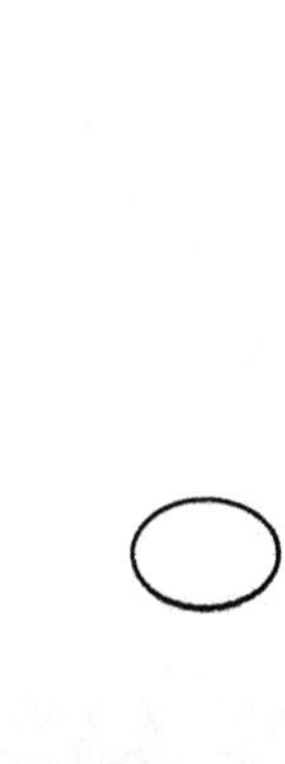

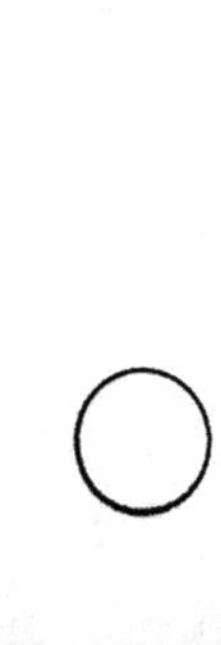

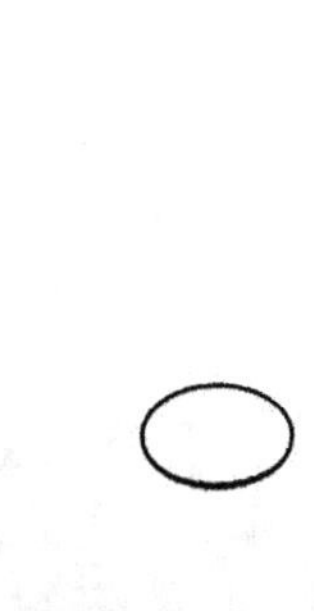

Time to get a new notebook